EMMANUEL JOSEPH

The Industry Dreamweavers, How Billionaires Turn Ideas into Empires That Span the Globe

Contents

1

Chapter 1: Genesis of a Dream

Beneath the polished veneer of every billionaire's empire lies a simple, unpolished dream. From the invention of a personal computer in a garage to the creation of a global e-commerce platform, these dreams have humble beginnings. Yet, they harbor the potential to revolutionize industries and reshape societies. Aspiring billionaires often start with a visionary spark—a solution to a pressing problem, an innovative product, or a groundbreaking service. They possess an unwavering belief in their ideas, regardless of the obstacles they face.

In the early stages, these dreamweavers navigate a labyrinth of challenges—limited resources, skepticism, and market competition. They embrace the risk and uncertainty inherent in entrepreneurship, demonstrating resilience and tenacity. Their dreams evolve through countless iterations, fueled by relentless passion and dedication. The genesis of a dream is not merely a moment of inspiration but a journey of continuous learning and adaptation.

Successful billionaires recognize the importance of building a strong foundation for their dreams. They invest in education, skill development, and networking to gain the knowledge and connections needed to turn their visions into reality. They seek mentors and collaborators who share their passion and can provide valuable insights and support. By fostering a culture of innovation and creativity, they create an environment where ideas can flourish.

As these dreamweavers take their first steps toward building their empires, they remain undeterred by initial setbacks. They view failures as opportunities for growth and learning, using them as stepping stones toward success. The genesis of a dream is a testament to the power of perseverance and the belief that even the grandest empires can emerge from the humblest beginnings.

2

Chapter 2: The Art of Visionary Thinking

Visionary thinking is the cornerstone of every billionaire's success story. It is the ability to see beyond the present and envision a future shaped by one's ideas and innovations. Visionary leaders possess a unique blend of creativity, strategic foresight, and the courage to challenge the status quo. They are not content with incremental improvements but strive for transformative change.

At the heart of visionary thinking is a deep understanding of market trends, consumer needs, and technological advancements. Billionaires immerse themselves in their industries, constantly seeking knowledge and staying ahead of the curve. They identify emerging opportunities and anticipate shifts in the market landscape. By doing so, they position themselves to capitalize on trends and drive innovation.

Visionary thinkers are adept at articulating their ideas and inspiring others to share their vision. They communicate their goals with clarity and conviction, rallying teams and stakeholders around a common purpose. Their passion and enthusiasm are infectious, motivating others to contribute to the realization of their vision. Visionary leaders foster a culture of collaboration and encourage diverse perspectives, recognizing that innovation thrives in an environment of collective creativity.

One of the defining characteristics of visionary thinkers is their willingness to take calculated risks. They understand that innovation often involves venturing into uncharted territory, where the outcome is uncertain. Yet, they embrace these risks with confidence, guided by a well-defined vision and strategic plan. By balancing risk with opportunity, they create a pathway to success and ensure their ideas have a lasting impact on the world.

3

Chapter 3: Building a Dream Team

No dream can be realized alone, and billionaires understand the importance of assembling a talented and dedicated team. Building a dream team requires identifying individuals who possess complementary skills, share the vision, and are committed to the mission. Billionaires invest time and effort in recruiting, developing, and retaining top talent, recognizing that their team's success is intrinsically linked to the success of their enterprise.

The process of building a dream team begins with defining the core values and culture of the organization. Billionaires establish a clear set of principles that guide their team's actions and decisions. These values create a sense of purpose and unity, fostering a positive and collaborative work environment. By promoting a culture of trust, transparency, and mutual respect, billionaires ensure that their team members are aligned with the organization's goals and values.

Recruitment is a critical aspect of team building, and billionaires are meticulous in their selection process. They seek individuals who not only possess the necessary skills and expertise but also demonstrate a passion for the mission. Billionaires prioritize diversity and inclusivity, recognizing that a diverse team brings a wealth of perspectives and ideas. They leverage various recruitment channels, including networking, referrals, and targeted outreach, to attract top talent.

Once the dream team is in place, billionaires focus on nurturing and developing their talent. They invest in training, mentorship, and professional development opportunities to ensure their team members have the resources and support they need to succeed. Billionaires also encourage a culture of continuous learning and innovation, empowering their team to take ownership of their work and contribute to the organization's growth. By building a dream team, billionaires create a foundation for sustained success and long-term impact.

4

Chapter 4: Crafting a Compelling Brand

A compelling brand is essential for turning an idea into a global empire. Billionaires understand that a strong brand identity sets their enterprise apart from competitors and resonates with consumers. Crafting a compelling brand involves defining the organization's core values, mission, and unique selling proposition. It requires a deep understanding of the target audience and their needs, preferences, and behaviors.

The process of brand-building begins with the creation of a distinctive brand identity. This includes developing a memorable logo, choosing a color palette, and designing a visual style that reflects the organization's personality. Billionaires invest in market research and consumer insights to ensure their brand identity aligns with the expectations and aspirations of their target audience. By creating a consistent and cohesive brand image, they establish a strong foundation for their marketing efforts.

A compelling brand goes beyond visual identity; it encompasses the entire customer experience. Billionaires focus on delivering exceptional products and services that meet or exceed customer expectations. They prioritize quality, reliability, and innovation, ensuring that their offerings stand out in the market. By consistently delivering value to customers, they build trust and loyalty, which are essential for long-term success.

Effective brand communication is another critical component of brand-building. Billionaires leverage various marketing channels, including social media, content marketing, and public relations, to promote their brand message. They engage with their audience through storytelling, highlighting the impact and benefits of their products and services. By creating authentic and meaningful connections with consumers, they cultivate a loyal customer base that advocates for their brand. Crafting a compelling brand is a continuous process that requires constant evaluation, adaptation, and innovation to stay relevant in a dynamic market landscape.

5

Chapter 5: Innovative Product Development

Innovation is at the heart of every successful enterprise, and billionaires excel at developing groundbreaking products that disrupt industries and captivate consumers. The process of innovative product development begins with identifying unmet needs and opportunities in the market. Billionaires conduct extensive research and gather insights from various sources, including consumer feedback, industry trends, and technological advancements.

Once a promising opportunity is identified, the focus shifts to ideation and concept development. Billionaires foster a culture of creativity and experimentation, encouraging their teams to brainstorm and explore new ideas. They leverage diverse perspectives and expertise to generate a wide range of concepts. The most promising ideas are then refined and developed into viable product prototypes.

The next stage involves rigorous testing and validation to ensure the product meets quality standards and delivers value to customers. Billionaires invest in state-of-the-art research and development facilities, where their teams conduct experiments, simulations, and user testing. They prioritize customer feedback and iterate on the product design based on real-world usage and insights. This iterative process ensures that the final product is not only innovative but also practical and user-friendly.

Successful product development also requires effective project management and execution. Billionaires establish clear timelines, milestones, and performance metrics to track progress and ensure timely delivery. They allocate resources efficiently and address any challenges or bottlenecks that arise. By maintaining a focus on quality, innovation, and customer satisfaction, billionaires bring groundbreaking products to market and create lasting impact.

6

Chapter 6: Strategic Market Entry

E ntering a new market is a critical phase for any aspiring billionaire, and it requires careful planning and execution. Strategic market entry involves assessing the target market's potential, identifying entry barriers, and developing a comprehensive market entry strategy. Billionaires conduct thorough market research to understand the competitive landscape, consumer preferences, and regulatory environment.

The first step in market entry is selecting the most appropriate entry mode. Billionaires evaluate various options, including exporting, licensing, franchising, joint ventures, and direct investment. Each entry mode has its advantages and risks, and the choice depends on factors such as market size, growth potential, and the level of control desired. Billionaires carefully weigh these factors and select the entry mode that aligns with their strategic objectives.

Once the entry mode is determined, the focus shifts to market positioning and differentiation. Billionaires develop a unique value proposition that sets their offerings apart from competitors. They craft tailored marketing and sales strategies to effectively communicate their value to the target audience. This may involve adapting products and services to meet local preferences, establishing partnerships with local distributors, and investing in localized marketing campaigns.

Successful market entry also requires navigating regulatory and legal complexities. Billionaires work closely with legal and compliance experts to ensure their operations adhere to local laws and regulations. They stay informed about changes in the regulatory environment and proactively address any compliance issues. By adopting a strategic and proactive approach to market entry, billionaires position themselves for success and establish a strong foothold in new markets.

7

Chapter 7: The Power of Networking

etworking is a vital component of every billionaire's success, providing access to valuable resources, opportunities, and relationships. Billionaires understand the importance of building and nurturing a robust professional network. They actively seek out connections with industry leaders, mentors, investors, and potential collaborators. These relationships serve as a source of support, guidance, and inspiration.

Building a powerful network begins with identifying key stakeholders and influencers in the industry. Billionaires attend conferences, seminars, and industry events to connect with like-minded individuals and expand their network. They also leverage online platforms and social media to engage with peers and thought leaders. By actively participating in industry discussions and sharing insights, billionaires position themselves as valuable contributors to their professional community.

Networking is not just about making connections but also about nurturing and maintaining relationships. Billionaires understand the importance of reciprocity and mutual support. They offer their expertise, resources, and assistance to others, creating a network built on trust and collaboration. By fostering meaningful relationships, they create a support system that provides valuable insights, opportunities, and partnerships.

Mentorship is another critical aspect of networking. Billionaires seek guidance from experienced mentors who have navigated similar challenges and achieved success in their fields. Mentors provide valuable advice, share lessons learned, and offer a fresh perspective on complex issues. Billionaires also pay it forward by mentoring aspiring entrepreneurs and sharing their knowledge and experiences with the next generation of leaders.

In addition to professional networking, billionaires recognize the value of building personal connections. They prioritize relationships with family, friends, and community members, understanding that a strong support system is essential for personal well-being and success. By balancing professional and personal networking, billionaires create a network that enriches their lives and contributes to their overall success.

8

Chapter 8: Strategic Partnerships and Collaborations

S trategic partnerships and collaborations play a crucial role in the growth and expansion of billion-dollar empires. Billionaires understand that no single entity can achieve greatness in isolation. They seek out partnerships that complement their strengths, fill gaps in their capabilities, and provide access to new markets and resources. These collaborations enable them to leverage synergies and create value that would be difficult to achieve independently.

The process of forming strategic partnerships begins with identifying potential collaborators who share similar goals and values. Billionaires conduct thorough due diligence to assess the compatibility and potential of each partnership. They consider factors such as the partner's reputation, track record, and strategic alignment with their vision. By carefully selecting partners, they ensure that the collaboration is built on a foundation of mutual trust and respect.

Successful collaborations require clear communication and well-defined roles and responsibilities. Billionaires establish open lines of communication with their partners, fostering a culture of transparency and accountability. They develop comprehensive partnership agreements that outline the objectives, expectations, and terms of the collaboration. These agreements serve as a roadmap for the partnership, ensuring that both parties are aligned and working towards common goals.

Billionaires also recognize the importance of nurturing and maintaining partnerships over time. They invest in building strong relationships with their partners, regularly reviewing the progress of the collaboration and addressing any challenges that arise. By fostering a spirit of cooperation and adaptability, they ensure that the partnership remains resilient and continues to create value in a dynamic business environment.

9

Chapter 9: Navigating Challenges and Adversity

E very journey to success is fraught with challenges and adversity, and billionaires are no exception. They encounter obstacles ranging from market volatility and regulatory hurdles to internal conflicts and personal setbacks. However, what sets them apart is their ability to navigate these challenges with resilience, adaptability, and a positive mindset.

One of the key strategies billionaires employ to overcome adversity is proactive risk management. They identify potential risks and develop contingency plans to mitigate their impact. This involves conducting thorough risk assessments, diversifying their investments, and building a robust crisis management framework. By anticipating and preparing for potential challenges, billionaires minimize disruptions and ensure business continuity.

Resilience is another critical trait that enables billionaires to navigate adversity. They maintain a positive outlook and view challenges as opportunities for growth and learning. Instead of being discouraged by setbacks, they embrace them as valuable lessons that inform their future decisions. This growth mindset allows them to bounce back from failures and continue pursuing their goals with renewed determination.

Adaptability is also essential for navigating challenges in a rapidly changing business landscape. Billionaires are quick to pivot and adjust their strategies in response to evolving market conditions and emerging trends. They stay informed about industry developments and continuously seek ways to innovate and improve their offerings. By remaining agile and flexible, they position themselves to seize new opportunities and stay ahead of the competition.

In addition to professional challenges, billionaires also face personal adversity. They prioritize their mental and physical well-being, recognizing that a healthy mind and body are essential for sustained success. They practice self-care, seek support from their loved ones, and engage in activities that bring them joy and fulfillment. By maintaining a balanced and holistic approach to life, billionaires build the resilience needed to overcome both personal and professional challenges.

10

Chapter 10: Scaling the Empire

Scaling an empire requires strategic planning, efficient execution, and a relentless focus on growth. Billionaires understand that expanding their business operations involves more than just increasing revenue; it requires building a scalable infrastructure, optimizing processes, and maintaining a strong organizational culture. By addressing these key areas, they position themselves for sustainable and long-term growth.

The first step in scaling an empire is to develop a comprehensive growth strategy. Billionaires identify new market opportunities, assess their competitive landscape, and set ambitious yet achievable goals. They prioritize investments in research and development, marketing, and talent acquisition to drive innovation and market penetration. By aligning their growth strategy with their core values and vision, they ensure that their expansion efforts are purposeful and impactful.

Building a scalable infrastructure is essential for supporting growth. Billionaires invest in advanced technologies, robust systems, and efficient processes that enable their organizations to handle increased demand and complexity. They focus on streamlining operations, improving supply chain management, and enhancing customer service. By creating a scalable infrastructure, they ensure that their organization can grow without compromising quality or performance.

Optimizing processes is another critical aspect of scaling an empire.

Billionaires continuously evaluate and refine their workflows to eliminate inefficiencies and maximize productivity. They implement best practices, leverage data analytics, and embrace automation to drive operational excellence. By fostering a culture of continuous improvement, they empower their teams to innovate and contribute to the organization's growth.

Maintaining a strong organizational culture is also crucial for scaling an empire. Billionaires recognize that their employees are their most valuable asset and prioritize their well-being and development. They invest in leadership training, employee engagement programs, and initiatives that promote diversity and inclusion. By fostering a positive and inclusive work environment, they ensure that their team remains motivated, committed, and aligned with the organization's goals. Scaling an empire is a complex and dynamic process, but with the right strategies and mindset, billionaires achieve remarkable growth and success.

11

Chapter 11: Strategic Innovation and Disruption

Billionaires are often synonymous with innovation and disruption. They possess a unique ability to identify opportunities for groundbreaking advancements and have the courage to challenge established norms. Strategic innovation involves not only developing new products and services but also reimagining business models, processes, and entire industries.

At the core of strategic innovation is a commitment to continuous improvement and a willingness to experiment. Billionaires foster a culture of innovation within their organizations, encouraging their teams to think creatively and embrace change. They allocate resources for research and development, providing the necessary tools and environment for innovative ideas to flourish. This culture of innovation extends to every aspect of their business, from product design and marketing to customer service and operations.

Disruption is often a byproduct of strategic innovation. By introducing new technologies or business models, billionaires can reshape entire industries and create new markets. Disruption requires a deep understanding of market dynamics and the ability to anticipate and respond to emerging trends. Billionaires leverage their knowledge and insights to identify gaps in the market and develop solutions that meet unmet needs. They also recognize that disruption can be met with resistance and are prepared to navigate challenges and pushback from established players.

One of the keys to successful innovation and disruption is staying ahead of the competition. Billionaires invest in competitive intelligence and market research to keep a pulse on industry trends and developments. They continuously monitor their competitors and adapt their strategies to maintain a competitive edge. By staying agile and proactive, they ensure that their innovations remain relevant and impactful in a rapidly changing business landscape.

12

Chapter 12: Financial Acumen and Investment Strategies

Financial acumen is a critical skill that enables billionaires to build and sustain their empires. They possess a deep understanding of financial principles, investment strategies, and risk management. This financial expertise allows them to make informed decisions, allocate resources effectively, and maximize returns on their investments.

One of the fundamental aspects of financial acumen is the ability to manage cash flow and capital. Billionaires prioritize financial stability and ensure that their businesses have sufficient liquidity to meet operational needs and invest in growth opportunities. They develop robust financial plans and budgets, carefully monitoring expenses and revenue streams. By maintaining a strong financial foundation, they create a platform for sustainable growth and expansion.

Investment strategies play a crucial role in wealth creation and preservation. Billionaires diversify their investment portfolios to minimize risk and optimize returns. They allocate capital across various asset classes, including equities, real estate, venture capital, and alternative investments. This diversification strategy allows them to capitalize on different market opportunities and hedge against potential losses. Billionaires also stay informed about market trends and economic developments, adjusting their investment strategies accordingly.

Risk management is another key component of financial acumen. Billionaires understand that every investment carries inherent risks and develop strategies to mitigate these risks. This involves conducting thorough due diligence, assessing potential risks, and implementing contingency plans. They also leverage insurance, hedging, and other risk management tools to protect their assets and ensure business continuity. By balancing risk and reward, billionaires create a resilient financial framework that supports long-term success.

13

Chapter 13: Philanthropy and Social Responsibility

Philanthropy and social responsibility are integral to the legacy of billionaires. They recognize that their success comes with a responsibility to give back to society and make a positive impact on the world. Billionaires engage in philanthropic activities and initiatives that address pressing social, environmental, and economic challenges. Their philanthropic efforts are driven by a sense of purpose and a commitment to creating lasting change.

Philanthropy often begins with identifying causes and issues that align with the billionaire's values and passions. They conduct thorough research to understand the needs and gaps in these areas and develop targeted strategies to address them. Billionaires leverage their financial resources, networks, and influence to support a wide range of initiatives, from education and healthcare to environmental conservation and poverty alleviation. Their philanthropic contributions go beyond financial donations, encompassing volunteerism, advocacy, and capacity-building efforts.

Social responsibility is also embedded in the business practices of billionaires. They prioritize ethical and sustainable operations, ensuring that their businesses contribute positively to society and the environment. This involves adopting fair labor practices, reducing environmental impact, and promoting diversity and inclusion. Billionaires also engage with stakeholders, including employees, customers, and communities, to create shared value and drive positive change. By integrating social responsibility into their business strategies, they build trust and credibility with stakeholders and enhance their overall impact.

One of the key principles of effective philanthropy is collaboration. Billionaires often partner with other organizations, governments, and communities to amplify their efforts and achieve greater impact. They recognize that complex social challenges require collective action and work collaboratively to develop innovative solutions. By fostering partnerships and leveraging their resources and expertise, billionaires create a powerful force for social good and drive meaningful change.

14

Chapter 14: Personal Growth and Development

Personal growth and development are essential for billionaires to achieve and sustain success. They are committed to continuous learning and self-improvement, recognizing that personal growth is the foundation for professional excellence. Billionaires invest in their own development, seeking opportunities to expand their knowledge, skills, and perspectives.

One of the key aspects of personal growth is lifelong learning. Billionaires prioritize education and actively seek out new knowledge and insights. They read extensively, attend conferences and seminars, and engage with thought leaders and experts in various fields. This commitment to learning enables them to stay informed about industry trends, technological advancements, and emerging opportunities. By continuously updating their knowledge and skills, billionaires position themselves to navigate the complexities of the business world and stay ahead of the competition.

Self-awareness is another critical component of personal growth. Billionaires engage in introspection and reflection to understand their strengths, weaknesses, and areas for improvement. They seek feedback from mentors, peers, and advisors, using this input to refine their strategies and behaviors. Self-awareness also involves recognizing and managing emotions, fostering resilience, and maintaining a positive mindset. By developing a deep sense of self-awareness, billionaires enhance their decision-making abilities and build strong, authentic relationships with others.

Personal growth also encompasses physical and mental well-being. Billionaires prioritize their health, recognizing that a healthy body and mind are essential for sustained success. They engage in regular exercise, maintain a balanced diet, and practice stress management techniques such as meditation and mindfulness. They also prioritize work-life balance, ensuring that they have time for family, friends, and personal interests. By taking care of their physical and mental well-being, billionaires build the energy and resilience needed to pursue their goals and overcome challenges.

15

Chapter 15: Legacy and Succession Planning

L egacy and succession planning are critical considerations for billionaires as they build and sustain their empires. They recognize that their impact extends beyond their lifetime and are committed to leaving a lasting legacy. Succession planning involves identifying and developing future leaders who can carry forward the vision and values of the organization. By planning for the future, billionaires ensure the continuity and longevity of their enterprises.

The process of legacy planning begins with defining the desired impact and values that will guide the billionaire's legacy. They articulate their vision for the future and identify key priorities and goals. This vision serves as a blueprint for the legacy they wish to leave behind. Billionaires also engage with stakeholders, including family members, employees, and community leaders, to gather input and build consensus around the legacy plan.

Succession planning involves identifying potential successors and preparing them for leadership roles. Billionaires assess the skills, experience, and potential of their leadership team, selecting individuals who align with the organization's values and vision. They invest in leadership development programs, mentorship, and coaching to equip future leaders with the knowledge and skills needed to succeed. This includes fostering a culture of continuous learning and development, where emerging leaders are encouraged to take on new challenges and responsibilities.

Effective succession planning also requires clear communication and transparency. Billionaires communicate their succession plan to key stakeholders, ensuring that everyone is aware of the future leadership structure and transition process. They also establish governance structures, such as boards and advisory councils, to provide oversight and guidance during the transition. By creating a clear and transparent succession plan, billionaires build trust and confidence in the future leadership of the organization.

Legacy planning also encompasses philanthropy and social impact. Billionaires establish foundations, endowments, and charitable organizations to support causes they are passionate about. They develop strategies to ensure that their philanthropic efforts continue to create positive change long after they are gone. By integrating legacy and succession planning into their overall strategy, billionaires create a lasting impact that extends beyond their lifetime and benefits future generations.

16

Chapter 16: Embracing Change and Adaptation

I n an ever-evolving business landscape, billionaires understand the importance of embracing change and adaptation. The ability to adapt to new circumstances, technologies, and market dynamics is a key factor in sustaining success. Billionaires are proactive in identifying emerging trends and opportunities, positioning themselves to capitalize on change and drive innovation.

One of the key principles of embracing change is a willingness to challenge the status quo. Billionaires are not complacent with existing practices and are always seeking ways to improve and innovate. They foster a culture of curiosity and experimentation within their organizations, encouraging their teams to explore new ideas and take calculated risks. This openness to change allows them to stay ahead of the competition and maintain their relevance in a rapidly changing world.

Adaptation also requires flexibility and agility. Billionaires are quick to pivot and adjust their strategies in response to shifting market conditions and customer preferences. They stay informed about industry developments and continuously monitor their performance and progress. By being adaptable and responsive, they ensure that their businesses remain competitive and resilient in the face of change.

Technology plays a significant role in driving change and adaptation. Billionaires invest in cutting-edge technologies and digital transformation initiatives to enhance their operations and offerings. They leverage data analytics, artificial intelligence, and automation to gain insights, improve efficiency, and deliver value to customers. By embracing technology, billionaires position themselves to harness the power of innovation and drive sustainable growth.

Embracing change also involves continuous learning and development. Billionaires prioritize their own growth and encourage their teams to do the same. They invest in training, workshops, and professional development programs to enhance their skills and knowledge. This commitment to learning ensures that they are well-equipped to navigate change and lead their organizations into the future.

Embracing change and adaptation also involves fostering a culture of resilience. Billionaires instill a sense of purpose and motivation within their teams, encouraging them to view challenges as opportunities for growth. They celebrate successes and learn from failures, creating an environment where continuous improvement is valued. By building a resilient and adaptive organization, billionaires ensure that they can thrive in a dynamic and uncertain world.

17

Chapter 17: The Legacy of the Dreamweavers

A s billionaires build and expand their empires, they leave behind a legacy that transcends their individual achievements. This legacy is not measured solely by financial success but by the positive impact they have on society, the innovations they introduce, and the lives they touch. The legacy of the dreamweavers is a testament to their vision, determination, and unwavering commitment to their dreams.

Billionaires recognize that their legacy is shaped by the values and principles they uphold. They prioritize ethical conduct, social responsibility, and environmental sustainability in their business practices. By integrating these values into their operations, they create a lasting impact that benefits future generations. Their legacy is also reflected in their philanthropic efforts, as they invest in initiatives that address critical social and environmental challenges.

The dreamweavers' legacy is also characterized by the inspiration and empowerment they provide to others. They serve as role models and mentors, sharing their knowledge and experiences to guide and inspire the next generation of entrepreneurs. Their stories of resilience, innovation, and success motivate others to pursue their own dreams and contribute to the betterment of society. By fostering a culture of entrepreneurship and innovation, billionaires create a ripple effect that extends far beyond their own achievements.

Ultimately, the legacy of the dreamweavers is a celebration of the human spirit and its boundless potential. It is a reminder that dreams, when pursued with passion and determination, have the power to change the world. As we reflect on the journeys of these visionary leaders, we are inspired to dream big, embrace challenges, and create our own lasting impact on the world.

Book Description: "The Industry Dreamweavers: How Billionaires Turn Ideas into Empires That Span the Globe"

In "The Industry Dreamweavers," embark on an inspiring journey through the minds and lives of billionaires who have transformed simple ideas into global empires. This captivating book delves into the secrets behind their success, exploring the visionary thinking, strategic innovation, and relentless determination that drive these extraordinary individuals.

Through 17 thought-provoking chapters, readers will uncover the genesis of a dream, the art of visionary thinking, and the power of building a dream team. The book highlights the importance of crafting a compelling brand, innovative product development, and strategic market entry. It also emphasizes the significance of networking, strategic partnerships, and navigating challenges with resilience and adaptability.

"The Industry Dreamweavers" sheds light on the financial acumen and investment strategies that billionaires employ to build and sustain their wealth. It explores their commitment to philanthropy and social responsibility, personal growth and development, and legacy and succession planning. The book concludes with a focus on embracing change and adaptation, ensuring long-term success in a dynamic world.

This insightful and engaging book serves as a guide for aspiring entrepreneurs, business leaders, and anyone with a dream to make a difference. By sharing the stories and lessons of the world's most successful billionaires, "The Industry Dreamweavers" inspires readers to dream big, think creatively, and turn their own ideas into impactful, world-changing realities.